A Christmas Treasury

a collection of joyful holiday readings

from

Our State
NORTH CAROLINA
Greensboro, N.C.

Published by *Our State* magazine, Greensboro, N.C.

A Christmas Treasury
copyright © 2006 by *Our State* magazine.
All rights reserved.
Published by *Our State* magazine, Mann Media Inc.
P.O. Box 4552, Greensboro, N.C. 27404
(800) 948-1409; www.ourstate.com
Printed in the United States by R.R. Donnelley & Sons

Library of Congress Cataloging-in-Publication Data

A Christmas treasury : a collection of joyful holiday readings from Our
State magazine.
    p. cm.
A collection of Christmas stories, quotes, and recipes drawn from the
73-year history of "Our State" magazine.
    ISBN 0-9779681-0-3 (pbk. : alk. paper)
    1. Christmas--Literary collections. 2. American literature--20th century.
3. Christmas--North Carolina--History. 4. North Carolina--Social life and
customs. 5. Christmas cookery. I. Our State (Greensboro, N.C.)
    PS509.C56C538 2006
    810.8'0334--dc22
                                        2006010600

TABLE OF CONTENTS

CHAPTER 1
Tall Tales

Since the days when Carl Goerch founded
The State magazine in 1933, stories that stretch the imagination
and tickle the funny bone have delighted our readers.

First, a Pear Tree

BY J.A.C. DUNN

I thought perhaps she'd give me a tie or an onyx steering wheel knob or a flask with built-in hairbrushes or something. But, no. On the first day of Christmas, right there in the living room was a potted pear tree with a partridge sitting in it.

An odd present. The pear tree might have borne fruit if planted, but I haven't planted it yet. At that moment I hadn't any idea what to do with the partridge either. It seemed a bit callous to eat my true love's Christmas present, particularly when it was given to me alive.

I moved the pear tree to a corner of the living room. The partridge didn't stir. In fact, it wouldn't even look at me.

I called her up. "Thanks very much for the pear tree and the partridge."

"I'm glad you like them," she said.

"I've always wanted one of each."

"I'm so happy," she said. "And thank you for the subscription to the *Vladivostock Herald*."

day 2   The next day, the postman brought a small box with holes in it. It was from her. Inside the box were two birds. The encyclopedia gave a description that matched them.

"Turtledove," it said, "noted for its plaintive cooing and affectionate disposition."

The turtledoves perched affectionately on the back of the armchair and cooed plaintively.

I called her up. "Thanks very much for the turtledoves. They're ... on the armchair right now."

"I'm glad you like them," she said. "I just thought I'd give you something else."

"What do you feed turtledoves?"

"Try turtles," she suggested. She has a literal mind.

day 3 The next afternoon, a delivery boy brought a slightly larger box, again with holes in it. Three hens huddled inside. One of them immediately made a mess on the hearth, and all three roosted on the mantelpiece, clucking idiotically.

I called her up. "Thanks for the hens."

"I thought you'd like them," she said. "They're French."

I gave the hens popcorn and offered some to the partridge. It ate sullenly, then turned its face to the wall again. The turtledoves cooed with plaintive enthusiasm but spurned popcorn.

day 4 Sign here," said the postman the next morning. He handed me a large box, again with holes. "What's this?"

"Dunno," he said. "Sounds like more birds. What're you starting, a zoo or something?"

"No," I said, "and anyway, the word is aviary."

The box did, indeed, contain more birds. Four of them. "Mockingbird," said the encyclopedia, "remarkable for its exact imitation of the notes of other birds."

Two of the mockingbirds joined the French hens on the mantelpiece and imitated them. A third joined the turtledoves

3

and cooed. The armchair was beginning to look streaky. The fourth mockingbird joined the partridge and turned its face to the wall.

I called her up. "There seem to be an awful lot of birds around here. Thanks, though. I like birds."

"Oh, I'm so glad. Maybe you could start a zoo?"

"You mean aviary," I said and went out to buy birdseed.

day 5 The postman rang again the next day.

"Birds?"

"Nope," said the postman. "Sign here."

The small package contained five gold rings, all different. I thought this a rather broad hint, coming from her. But at least they weren't birds.

I called her.

"Beautiful rings. Thank you."

Her reply was very demure.

day 6 I don't understand why you keep sending me presents," I said to her the next day. "It's not that I don't appreciate them or anything, but I should have thought that just one gift ..."

"Don't you like the geese?"

"Great geese," I said. "Love the geese. They just arrived. The trouble is they keep laying eggs all over the place. One of them's been laying in the bathtub, and I keep having to clean goose egg out of the drain."

"I'm sorry if they're a bother," she said sweetly. "I just wanted ..."

day 7 The following morning, four men marched up the driveway carrying a large inflated plastic wading pool. They set it on the front porch, filled it with water, and then produced from a large box (with holes) seven swans. They put the swans in the wading pool.

I stood mutely watching this operation, and when it was finished, one of the men shook his head sadly at me, and they went away.

"Look," I said to her over the telephone, "I'm very grateful for all you've done, but how about easing off on the birds? I've got 23 now, and this is a pretty small house. Besides, swans bite."

She sounded so injured I hadn't the heart to suggest that she stop sending presents altogether.

day 8   I wish I had. The next day eight girls of coed age came to the door dressed in full skirts and peasant blouses.

"We're here," said one when I answered the knock.

"Who are you?"

"Maids. We've come to milk." She curtsied.

I called up my true love. "Now look," I said sternly. "Fun's fun and all that, but these maids, now …"

"Don't you like maids-a-milking?"

"The maids are fine; it's the cows they brought that present a problem. I haven't the space for — oh, never mind." She had begun to grow tearful.

The maids took their cows to the backyard and milked. I fed the birds, bought hay for the cows, laid in a stock of TV dinners for the maids. Then I killed the partridge and cooked it. It was getting on my nerves, brooding in the pear tree while everything else was cooing or clucking or mocking or laying or swimming.

I decided the maids could help eat the steadily increasing supply of goose eggs, which had turned out to be unmarketable.

By this time my dog, a neurotic basset, had retreated to the hall closet and was eyeing activities with a quivering lip.

But she wasn't finished.

day 9 At about four the next afternoon, the correct hour for calling, nine fashionably dressed ladies appeared at the front door.

"We're here," said the leading lady.

"Why?"

"We've come to wait," said the leading lady.

"Wait for what?" I asked, but they all walked right past me into the living room, where they sat down and started waiting.

"My, what a lot of birds," said one. "May I have a cigarette?"

I gave her one and flew to the telephone. "What are you trying to do to me?" I quavered. "I'm not a rich man, and here I have 48 mouths to feed, not counting my own. There are 17 strange women in the house. The place is going wild. Stop, will you? I know you love me. If you want to send me presents, send me a tie or an onyx steering wheel knob."

She began to cry. I didn't care about her, I didn't appreciate the love she was trying to show, I was heartless, cruel ...

day 10 The next morning, I was awakened at six by pounding. On the front porch were 10 men in brocaded costumes, leaping. The swans snapped at them whenever they got within range of the pool. I hurried outside, panicked.

"What's all this?"

"Lords," said one of the men laconically, in the middle of a powerful flamenco stamp. "Come to leap." He leapt, proving it.

"Oh, no. How long do you plan to stay?"

"Contract reads 13 weeks, with option," said the leading lord, and he performed a flying split.

"Come in," I said, wearily. "Let me introduce you to some

6

waiting ladies."

"Hey, hear that, fellas? GIRLS!"

They all leapt and pirouetted through the door, and almost immediately the living room sounded like a cocktail party in full swing. As a matter of fact, later in the day it became just that, with a lord occasionally springing up, highball in hand, to do a spin or an entrechat.

day 11 I hocked the five golden rings, bought 27 TV dinners, more hay, birdseed, 10-gallon cans to keep the cows' milk in, and extra towels. Then I went to work. At work, I got a telephone call from the police.

"Buncha guys on your porch havin' some sort of jam session," said the desk sergeant. "Thought you oughta know. Wunna my men talked to 'em, they said they was suppos'ta be there. What's it all about?"

I HURRIED HOME ...

Eleven men sat on the front porch.

"We're pipers," said one. He was wearing sideburns and sandals. "Like, we're gonna pipe for you, man." They were all propped against this or that or each other, tooting on recorders. They wore blue jeans and sweat shirts, and one had a bad cough.

"How long?" I asked.

"Who knows? Till we fade, I guess. Great pad you got here."

EPILOGUE

I got a room in a motel. I didn't even call her up. When I left, the cows had run dry, and the maids and ladies were all reading magazines in the living room, while the lords and pipers had a ball throughout the house.

Two or three lord-lady romances were budding; the armchair was encrusted; the bathtub drain was hopelessly clogged; the cows, clustered hungrily at the back door, were anxiously disturbing the peace; the swans attacked anybody who approached their pool; one of the mockingbirds had abandoned the French hens and was imitating the pipers, another had deserted the turtledoves and was imitating the cows; the French hens had nested in the laundry hamper; the pear tree was beginning to wilt; the spare towels had run out; and the dog had had a nervous breakdown and run away, gibbering.

I don't know what she'll send me tomorrow, but if it makes any more noise, I'm simply going to have to leave town. My landlord has threatened to raise the rent, and after all, with 38 extra people, 22 birds, eight cows, and an extra tree on the property, can you blame him?

—*Previously published in* The State, *December 15, 1965.*

Post-Holiday Blues

The day after Christmas — back to the grind,
Christmas joy and laughter all behind;
The remnants of turkey, mince pie, and cake
Clutter up the pantry and seem awful to take.

The gifts which yesterday seemed gorgeous and fine
Now look a bit shoddy — like an old Valentine;
The hose are too dark, the gloves are too small,
And most of the things I don't care for at all.

The rooms must be straightened, the tree must come down,
For a single day's pleasure we pay with a frown.
Why don't we celebrate the whole week through,
And January first start the year all anew?

— LAURA VIRGINIA SNUGGS
Previously published in The State, *January 25, 1940.*

Too Many Santa Clauses

By Carl Goerch

The setting for this tale is in a country school not far from the town of Lenoir in Watauga County.

A couple of weeks before last Christmas, teachers and other members of the Parent Teacher Association decided to put on a rip-snortin' Christmas program. Word leaked out about plans and preparations, and all the children got tremendously interested.

One of the first things the kids wanted to know was whether Santa Claus was going to be present. They were informed that a letter had been set to Santa at the North Pole, but nobody could be exactly sure whether he would show up or not.

The children hoped and prayed that he would.

Three or four of the grown-ups got together and decided that Santa would have to be present by all means, otherwise there would be a lot of disappointment.

"Let's get Jim Walker to dress up," someone suggested.

They went to call on Mr. Walker, a middle-aged farmer who lived about a mile from the school. He didn't much want to do it, but they finally persuaded him to accept.

"Tell Mrs. Walker to make you a Santa Claus suit," they suggested. "All you have to do is stand around and let the children see you and help distribute the presents."

Mr. Walker said OK.

Several other grown-ups, not knowing what the first group had done, called on Mr. Tom Hadley with the same proposition. "We want you to act as Santa Claus at the Christmas celebration," they informed him. "Don't say anything about it, because we want this to be a big surprise to the children."

"Well, I don't know much about how to do it, but if the kids have got to have a Santa Claus, I reckon it's up to me to help out," he stated. "I'll get my wife to make me some kind of suit to wear at the celebration."

Here comes Santa Claus

The event was to be held on the night of December 21. The children were still debating whether or not Santa Claus would put in an appearance. Teachers and parents continued to keep them in suspense. The adults knew that preparations had been made to have a Santa Claus present, but they didn't know that a duplication had inadvertently been arranged.

When the program started at 8 o'clock, the school auditorium was packed and jammed with children and grown-ups. The school orchestra rendered several selections. There was an appropriate Christmas talk by the preacher. And then — in walked Mr. Walker, dressed in a perfectly nifty Santa Claus suit!

The children applauded joyously. Santa had come all the way from the North Pole to pay them a visit. They cheered him for several minutes, and Mr. Walker bowed and waved his hand at them.

Just a second, Santa

And now, momentarily, we turn to Mr. Hadley.

It was close to Christmas. Mr. Hadley felt that the advent of the Yuletide season justified him in taking a drink. So he drank a toast to himself. Then he dressed up in the suit his wife had

11

made for him.

He surveyed himself proudly in the glass and decided it would be polite and considerate to drink a toast to Santa Claus, too, which he thereupon proceeded to do.

Just as he was leaving the house, he happened to think of Mrs. Santa Claus, 'way up there at the North Pole — poor old lady — so he drank a toast to her, too. And then, as a final thought, he also remembered the reindeer.

All of which meant that by the time he arrived at his destination, he was in a highly festive mood.

FACE OFF

He entered the back door of the auditorium and walked out on the platform.

The children gasped in amazement. They hadn't been sure whether one Santa Claus would show up or not, and here — all of a sudden — were two of them.

They yelled, stamped their feet, and clapped their hands.

Mr. Hadley bowed in appreciation of the reception being accorded him. Then he happened to look over toward the side of the stage and saw Mr. Walker.

An interloper!

He walked somewhat unsteadily over toward Mr. Walker and said, "What are you doing here?"

"I'm Santa Claus," said Mr. Walker.

"No you're not," said Mr. Hadley. "I'm Santa Claus."

"I was here first."

"Yes, and you're going to get out of here first."

The children sat with eyes and mouths wide open.

"I'm not," said Mr. Walker. "You've got no business here, and besides, you're drunk."

Mr. Hadley looked around him. Members of the school orchestra had left their instruments on the stage. A guitar was within easy reaching distance. He grabbed it, held it firmly in his right hand, took a long swing, and crowned Mr. Walker with it.

The guitar burst into pieces. Mr. Walker staggered back from the blow. The children went wild. They didn't know what it was all about, but they were having the time of their lives.

"You — you — you —" gulped Mr. Walker. And then he called Mr. Hadley something that little children aren't supposed to hear, but they heard and, naturally, were delighted. Mr. Walker reached over on a table, picked up a book, and slung it at Mr. Hadley. He socked him squarely in the face with it.

Then Mr. Hadley started cussing. The children discovered that he was even more fluent than the other Santa Claus. The latter started forward and landed a blow on Mr. Hadley's face. Mr. Hadley took a wild swing and missed.

"Sock him, Santa!"

"Kill him, Santa Claus!"

"In the belly, Santa! Hit 'im in the belly!"

The entire auditorium was in an uproar. The two Santa Clauses were going at each other with everything they had. Four or five men sprang from their seats and went up on the platform. They succeeded in separating the combatants. They ushered them unceremoniously out of the building and told them to stay there and not come back in again.

ALL'S WELL THAT END'S WELL

Then the school principal said that in view of unforeseen circumstances, he himself would enact the part of Santa Claus. The kids didn't give a rap about the rest of the program. They had seen enough to last them a lifetime, and they haven't quit talking yet about the dandy fight that Santa Claus and his brother put on for them.

— *From* Down Home, *by Carl Goerch, published 1943.*

"Riding the Fantastic"

United States Senator Clyde Hoey mentioned "riding the fantastic," an old Christmas custom he used to participate in.

"When I was a boy 7 or 8 years old, riding the fantastic was one of the outstanding things in observing Christmas around Shelby. Scores of people would dress up in all sorts of outlandish costumes and false faces. Then they'd get on a horse and proceed to ride all over town, cut all sorts of capers, sing Christmas songs, and everybody in town always turned out to watch the fun.

"It would last for two or three hours, and then the crowds would disperse and go home for Christmas dinner.

"I believe it had sort of died out about the time I got to be 15 years old."

—Previously published in The State, *December 10, 1949.*

Just for a Visit

By Carl Goerch

The Christmas season is at its height!

During the past week, the stores have been thronged with eager shoppers, and there's been an air of excitement and tenseness everywhere. There's been the customary rush of getting everything in readiness around the house: tying up packages, fixing decorations, arranging for the Christmas dinner, and other things of that nature.

There's the early awakening on Christmas morning, the fun of distributing gifts, and perhaps a few visits before noon. And then, there's the big turkey dinner with all its trimmings from soup to nuts. And after that...

It's about the "after that" period we want to talk about.

A LET-DOWN FEELING

Following all that excitement, there's always a sort of let-down feeling in evidence after dinner. The chances are that you've been up late Christmas Eve, fixing the tree, getting gifts ready or attending a party at some friend's home. You've also had to get up early on Christmas morning, because the children would resent it if you stayed in bed. So it's perfectly natural that you should be rather worn out when you get up from the dinner table. Worn out, but perfectly happy, contented and satisfied.

I don't know about you, but there's only one thing I'm good for on occasions like that, and that is to go upstairs and take a nap. There's nothing more blissful than stretching out on bed and realizing that you've got nothing to do for the next few hours and nothing to worry about.

There's only one ogre to bother you, only one nemesis to disrupt the peace and quiet of the afternoon, only one annoyance to cause you to worry — and that's the doorbell.

Just as you stretch out comfortably, giving a deep sigh of contentment and closing your eyes, the doorbell is apt to ring. You have to get up, run downstairs, open the door, and discover that it's Mr. and Mrs. Dingrimple, come to pay a Christmas afternoon visit.

They stay for half an hour. You have difficulty in keeping your eyes open, and you try your darndest to make your conversation interesting and entertaining, but it's a difficult task to accomplish.

Finally they leave. You go back upstairs again. You stretch out once more on your comfortable bed, and you get about halfway asleep, when the blasted bell rings again.

It's Mr. and Mrs. Whangdoodle this time, and it's the same thing all over again.

I don't know of anything that can be more worrisome. Of course, you're glad to have your friends call on you, but there are times when a nice nap for an hour or so seems more desirable than a visit from even your closest friends.

ONE OF THOSE TIMES

So far as I can recall, the only perfect Christmas afternoon I've ever spent in all my life was down in Washington about six or seven years ago. My wife and I had been to a party on Christmas Eve at the Jesse Harringtons. We got home about midnight. The tree still had to be decorated, and the presents for the children had to be arranged underneath. It was well after one o'clock before we finally retired.

The children were considerably younger then. They woke up at about six o'clock, and there was nothing for us to do but get up with them. Then followed the excitement of opening up the gifts. Later in the morning, we called on a dozen or more friends. Just before noon, I went down to the Keys Hotel for a glass of that famous eggnog that Mr. Keys knows how to make so well. He always has about 20 of his friends as his guests at that time.

Then back home again for dinner, and after dinner I prepared to lie down and relax.

Suddenly, however, I recalled past experiences with the doorbell. I knew that it wouldn't be long before the bell would start its infernal ringing and that my Christmas afternoon would be completely broken up.

And then it was that I was struck with one of those bright ideas that come to us only once or twice in a lifetime. I remembered that one of Jim Hackney's children, next door, had been suffering from diphtheria and had been well only a few days. I went over to Jim's house and asked him whether he still had the yellow quarantine sign. He found it back in the kitchen and gladly let me have it.

I went back to our house, got some tacks, and affixed the sign to our front door. Then I went back in the living room, stretched out on the the davenport, and proceeded to go to sleep.

A BLISSFUL AFTERNOON

And do you know that I slept for almost three hours without a single interruption? It was positively the most glorious nap I've ever had, and when I woke up at last, I felt like a new man.

The children told me what had happened in the meanwhile. Four or five cars had driven up, people had climbed out and had started up the walk. At the bottom of the porch steps they had

17

observed the quarantine sign. A moment's conversation. They then had promptly turned around, got back into their cars again, and had driven off.

I'm passing the idea on to you, and you can make use of it this Christmas afternoon if you want to without any cost whatsoever. However, it's best not to tell your wife about it until afterwards. Mine raised cane when she found out, but it was too late then to do anything about it.

— *Previously published in* The State, *December 25, 1937.*

CHAPTER 2

Traditions

Times and technology have changed since the days when North Carolina was a colony, and some of our Christmas traditions are rooted in a forgotten past.

Teacher Lock Out

BY SAMUEL E. LEONARD

Before the turn of the [past] century and several years thereafter, North Carolina was dotted with one-room, one-teacher schoolhouses from Murphy to Manteo. Only the larger towns had schools with grades and multiple teachers. Many of the one-room schools were of log construction; and in 1891, when I was a lad of six, I went to a log schoolhouse in upper Davidson County.

Later, in 1905-06, I taught a one-teacher school. I had up to 65 pupils a day with books from ABCs to algebra. The school ran for four months, and I was paid $135 in a lump sum at the end of the term.

In those days, it was customary for the teacher to give a "treat" to the pupils just before Christmas. This consisted of a few sticks of candy, some raisins, or fruit. It was likewise customary to ask the teacher sometime in December if he were going to "treat." Of course, he knew he would, but oftentimes he said "no" just to see what would happen.

The teacher had a large handbell, which he rang at the door to call the pupils in the morning, at recess, lunch, or anytime school was not in session, which the pupils called "books." After the teacher said "no," the pupils would conspire together and watch for a time when he was out of the schoolhouse and the bell on the inside. The idea was to "lock the teacher out," that is to close the door (the schoolhouse had only one door) and not let him in to get the bell. Without the bell, he could not call the pupils in.

This was an exciting time, with the teacher shaking the door, trying to get in a window, and threatening all kinds of things if the door was not opened. Some of the little ones were usually scared and crying, but if the larger boys stuck to it and the teacher finally said he would "treat," the door was opened, the bell was run, and school was resumed as usual.

UNINFORMED

It so happened one year that the school teacher was a cousin of mine. He later went to college and seminary and became a Methodist preacher. My older brother was one of the big boys at the school and asked the teacher if he were going to "treat" for Christmas. The teacher said "no," but he didn't know what he was in for. When the time came that the teacher was out of the schoolhouse, the door was closed, and my brother stood guard at the door. The teacher came and shook the door, tried the windows, and made all sorts of threats, but the bigger boys stood firm. Still, the teacher said "no."

There was a big red mudhole in the road in front of the schoolhouse, and with my brother as leader, the boys tackled the teacher, brought him down, and started carrying him to the mudhole. I remember, as a little boy, holding a foot as we moved toward the road. The teacher realized he was beaten, and he said "yes" to save himself from the mudhole. He was turned loose, went into the house, rang the bell, and the incident was over.

It took quite some time to get things settled down, but there were no reprisals. And we got our "treat."

— *Previously published in* The State, *December 1976.*

When School Boys Fought for Holidays

O   ne of the most outstanding visitors to the state who
        had the ability to observe and record the things he
        saw in a fairly objective manner was a Philadelphia
merchant named William Attmore. The merchant came to
North Carolina in the winter of 1878 to collect debts owed to
his firm.

One of his first recorded observations, dated Thursday,
December 20, dealt with the strange manner in which Tar
Heel school boys of that day went about securing Christmas
vacations.

In his journal, Attmore wrote:

*We were alarmed in our quarters before day, by the
firing of muskets at some little distance from the house
in which we lay — We found that the firing was at a
schoolhouse in the neighborhood of our quarters with
powder only; tis the custom here for school boys upon the
approach of Christmas, Easter, and Whitsuntide, to rebel
against their schoolmaster in order to force him to grant
them a holiday. The boys rise early in the morning and
go to the schoolhouse which is considered as their fort,
they barricade the door and windows, carry into the*

house with them victuals and blankets, with water and wood, sufficient to sustain the siege that they expect from the master. Upon his approach at the usual school hour, he finds himself shut out, he demands the cause, the garrison acquaints him that they are determined to have a holiday, this is frequently denied, and now commences the siege, the master tries to force his way into the house, they resist him by every means in their power, and sometimes give him some very hard knocks, throw stones, etc.

It is generally looked upon as a piece of fun; the master pretends to be solicitous to subdue them, and if he catches any straggler from the fort, he will flog him heartily, and it is understood on these occasions that the boys are to be peaceable except during the actual storm of the enemy, when they are at liberty to maul him to their hearts content. ...

This scene is sometimes continued many days, at last the master proposed terms, that he grants them so many days holiday, which is satisfactory being accepted by the garrison, peace is again established in the little community.

The mere fact that the visiting merchant took note of this procedure would certainly indicate that it was peculiar to this section of the country and not a commonplace ritual throughout the entire country.

Attmore, however, did not limit his observations to this single curiosity. Under the heading of Sunday, December 23, he made the following entry in his journal:

It is very much the custom in North Carolina to drink drams of some kind or other before breakfast, sometimes gin, cherry-bounce, eggnog, etc. Several of the assembly-men this morning indulged themselves in this respect.

Attmore was evidently quite impressed with North Carolina eggnog, for on Tuesday, December 25, he entered the following note in his journal:

This morning, according to North Carolina custom, we had before breakfast a drink of eggnog, this compound is made in the following manner: In two clean quart bowls were divided the yolks and whites of five eggs, the yolks and whites separated, the yolks beat up with a spoon and mixed up with brown sugar, the whites were whisk'd into froth by a straw whisk till the straw wou'd stand upright in it; when duly beat the yolks were put to the froth; again beat a long time; then a half a pint of Rum pour'd slowly into the mixture, the whole kept stirring the whole time till well incorporated.

— *Previously published in* The State, *December 10, 1960.*

No Harm in Merrymaking

O ur town authorities on Christmas generally let the boys
have their own way so far as mere noise is concerned,
although order in all essential particulars was enforced. There
was, therefore, much firing of crackers, rockets, sarpients, etc.,
and a good deal of cheering and shouting, but nothing worse,
and as the night wore on and even ceased, the town slept.

— Wilmington Journal, *December 29, 1859.*

Old Christmas

BY W.B. WRIGHT

The celebration of Old Christmas, observed 11 days after December 25th, persisted longer in North Carolina than in most states, particularly in the isolated mountain and coastal regions. And on the Outer Banks at Rodanthe — no longer remote — Old Christmas is still celebrated in early January, an event that has lately attracted attention of the media. But such celebrations are rare.

A notable exception occurred in Swansboro, January 6-7, 1983, when that pretty coastal town was observing its 200th anniversary. The late Tucker Littleton, well-remembered by *The State* readers, headed an authentic Old Christmas observance, and in the Souvenir Booklet [included] an account that may help new generations understand the old ways:

> *"The adoption of the Gregorian calendar by England in 1752 and its application to her 13 American colonies not only left the masses of the common people puzzled by the complicated mathematical calculations used to prove the validity of the new calendar, but it also occasioned a very considerable religious controversy over which date was the true Christmas.*
>
> *"December 25 had been established as the date for*

Christmas in the 4th century, and that, of course, was according to the old calendar put in effect long before Julius Caesar. When the Gregorian calendar was adopted by England, it continued to designate Christmas as December 25. But the problem was this: The corrections made by the Gregorian calendar caused December 25 to come 11 days earlier in 1752 than it could have come under the old Julian calendar. In other words, the day that would have been December 25 under the old calendar did not arrive under the new calendar until January 6th. ...

"Even popular superstitions had arisen to add support for Old Christmas. Ask some unfortunate mother who had irreverently disregarded the prohibition against changing the bedding and bed linens between the Christmases, and she could tell you. What the old folks had told her would happen did. For any household in which the bed linens were changed between December 25 and January 6 would lose a member by death. ... It is no marvel that Old Christmas in the isolated coastal communities of North Carolina remained a strong tradition for most of our history.

"Old Christmas, as it was observed in North Carolina before the Civil War, was purely a religious and social event, restricted largely to one's family and immediate circle of close friends. It was a time for feasting, sharing, and spending one's time with loved ones, and focusing a reverent attention upon the Biblical events of the Nativity. In startling contrast to modern traditions, Old Christmas had no Christmas tree, no lights, no Santa Claus, no Christmas cards, and no over-extending of the family budget to buy a lot of very expensive gifts for a lot of people.

"Instead, Old Christmas traditions included such events as the lighting of the Yule log; the singing of the ancient carols; the decorating of the house with natural greenery, berries, and fruit; the burning of candles in the windows; and *the hanging of one stocking for each child in the family.*

"The kitchen, where Old Christmas preparations centered, was filled with the special aroma of the season. Along with the other foods, there were the ones often enjoyed only at Christmastime, such as fruitcake, sillabub, eggnog, raisin pies, and similar delights. On the coast, it became a tradition to have an outdoor oyster roast sometime during Old Christmas day. And somewhere during all the festive events, there had to be time for some traditional dances.

"In the earlier years, it was traditional for the community on Old Christmas morning to be awakened by the sound of fife and drum, as the local musicians would march through the pre-dawn streets playing the familiar ancient Christmas tunes. Later in the 19th and early 20th centuries, this custom was replaced by the firing of guns here and there to wake up one's family and neighbors."

One more note, the date for Old Christmas — once set at January 6 — has now moved to January 7 [until the year 2100] because the difference between the solar year and the old Julian calendar is a progressive discrepancy. The length of time between December 25 and Old Christmas will slowly continue to widen.

— Previously published in The State, *December 1984.*

An Outer Banks Christmas

By Thomas Yocum

L ong before they had paved roads or national seashores, residents of the Outer Banks relished the celebration of Christmas — hailed as a special time to put aside the daily struggles of coastal life; enjoy a feast, eggnog, or maybe a bit of moonshine; play games or dance the night away; and gather with friends and family to celebrate the holiday season. Christmas was so popular, in fact, residents observed it twice — once on December 25 and again on January 6.

And that's only one of several holiday traditions unique to North Carolina's 130 miles of barrier islands.

TWO FOR THE PRICE OF ONE

The tale of the two Christmases began in 1752 when England adopted the Gregorian calendar. The switch eliminated 11 days from the calendar, something the independent Outer Bankers were loath to do. They kept their Christmas — Old Christmas — on January 6, as it had always been.

But when they began to see how much the rest of the world enjoyed the new one on December 25, they added that one, too.

Historians say the isolated, seabound culture imbued its residents with a distinct set of traditions. "Because this was a maritime place, there used to be a fair amount of traffic in and out of the inlets," explained Wynne Dough, [the first] director of the Outer Banks History Center in Manteo. "People traveled to Trinidad and Liverpool and Barbados as much as they did to places such as Baltimore, so it was fairly cosmopolitan. A lot of the people who shipped out were fairly widely traveled."

Dough said Old Christmas may have been a solemn and religious day for some, but for most islanders, it was a time to relax and enjoy. "Old Christmas was a time for secular blessings on fruit trees or for venturing outside in the small hours to watch livestock kneel in remembrance of the nativity; but dancing, feasting, gift-giving, and other practices common today had no clear religious import.

"On Hatteras Island, loose bands went from house to house on Old Christmas, frequently in disguise, making raucous music, and soliciting food and drink. Leaders of the processions sometimes carried a pole topped with the head of a cow or a steer, very likely one butchered for a common meal, and this mascot evolved into Old Buck — one or more revelers in a roughly made bovine costume, which has become a symbol of the holiday.

"Hatteras Island celebrations probably derived from English Christmas merrymaking and Scottish Hogmanay, of New Year's customs, but they also bore a superficial resemblance to John Kuner, a winter festival of African origin. John Kuner, also known as Jonkonnu, featured roving groups of masked participants and a leader in a horned headdress, called the 'rag man.' John Kuner was widely observed in the West Indies but remained virtually unknown in the United States outside eastern North Carolina and southeastern Virginia. White mainlanders are known to have gone 'kunering' for novelty in the 19th century, so a casual link with Old Christmas is possible."

To catch a husband

The Outer Banks and the nearby mainland were also home to other bygone traditions. "In the Dare County community of Stumpy Point, and perhaps elsewhere, girls and unmarried women sometimes set out a meal at a 'dumb table' on the eve of Old Christmas hoping to catch the apparitions of their future husbands hovering over empty places. This custom may be connected with St. Agnes' Eve, on January 20, when legend says that women dream of their future husbands," Dough said.

Another folk belief, shared elsewhere in the South, held that ashes from the stove or heater had to be kept inside between December 25 and January 6. According to legend, if the ashes were taken out, a corpse was sure to be taken out the same way before too long.

"There's a bit of a paradox at work here," said Dough. "On one hand, the people were conservative because they clung to Old Christmas. On the other hand, they seem to have taken a variety of observances and run them through the proverbial Cuisinart and come up with a blend of traditions. Observances such as Old Christmas, New Christmas, and some of the other traditions were social as well as religious events in a place where there wasn't a whole lot of social life."

A FINE FEAST INDEED

Historic celebrations of the current December 25 date for Christmas gradually adopted a more contemporary look, but they still maintained a decidedly different Outer Banks flair. In the weeks and days before the holiday, residents gathered mistletoe and packed it in barrels, which were shipped and sold in places such as New York. The barrels came back filled with clothes and other items that soon found their way under local Christmas trees.

Women fixed box lunches and desserts to sell to make money for Christmas programs, while the men slaughtered hogs and chopped enough wood so they wouldn't have to perform any chores for a few days. Bacon, sausage, salted hams, and smoked pork shoulders were prepared, and a thick pork tenderloin set aside for Christmas Day. "Hog Killing Stew," a recipe made from fresh hog hearts and livers, some lean pork, turnips, onions, potatoes, and corn dumplings, was a favorite meal for many Outer Banks families.

On Christmas Eve, Outer Banks residents held a big dance, and everyone turned out for a party that often lasted until dawn. Then, they returned to the smell of freshly baked cakes and pies in their sturdy little houses decorated with holly and mistletoe. On Christmas morning, children found stockings stuffed — hanging from the chimney — and a few simple gifts. On Christmas night, families enjoyed a feast of pork and fresh goose harvested from the sound.

OLD BUCK STOPS HERE

The traditions of Old Christmas and its wily and sometimes fierce mascot, Old Buck, are still alive on Hatteras Island. While most children in North Carolina hope for a visit from Santa Claus, children of some families on northern Hatteras Island look forward to the appearance of Old Buck — and Christmas treats.

"Old Buck faithfully makes his appearance every Old Christmas, to the delight of the island children, particularly those around Rodanthe and Avon, so that he can report on them each time Christmas rolls around," remembered the late Outer Banks storyteller Charles Whedbee in his book *Outer Banks Mysteries*. "He is a reliable source for the gift-giving adults who want to know which children have been really good for a whole year and which ones might not have been so good."

This year, Old Buck will again peer out from the deepest and darkest woods of Hatteras Island, watching the island children and taking note of who's naughty and nice. He'll most likely make an appearance at an Old Christmas celebration, and when he does, he'll continue a tradition that began more than two centuries ago on the windswept islands of the Outer Banks, when the calendar lost 11 days, but the people gained an extra Christmas.

— *Previously published in* Our State, *December 1999.*

Candles by Miss Ella

BY MAJEL IVEY SEAY

M iss Ella" is making candles, which is a definite harbinger of Christmas just as surely as the robin is a harbinger of spring.

"Miss Ella," to be more explicit, is Miss Ella Butler of the Moravian settlement of Old Salem, the twin city of Winston. For about two months before Christmas, Miss Ella busies herself with her annual task of making by hand, in exactly the same moulds and in exactly the same manner as they were made in 1766, the more than 10,000 candles used for the Moravian Christmas Love Feast, observed by all the churches of the Southern Moravian Province comprising North Carolina and Virginia.

For this enormous task, which Miss Ella performs with loving preciseness and care, approximately 90 pounds of tallow and 300 pounds of beeswax are used. After being melted in large vessels having the appearance of coffee pots, the tallow and wax are poured into the century-and-a-half old moulds, some of which contain six candles, others as many as 12.

As a final, colorful touch to the candles, Miss Ella arranges confetti-like paper around their bases and then stores them carefully away for the celebrated Love Feast observed on Christmas Eve.

— *Previously published in* The State, *December 16, 1939.*

Christmas Noise

By Bill Sharpe

In earlier days, when homes in rural North Carolina were widely scattered, citizens early on Christmas morning would fire their rifles and pistols as a greeting to their far-away neighbors. These would take up the firing and so spread the "merry Christmas" noise throughout the land. Firecrackers gradually replaced the firearms as noise-makers.

The custom seems to have died out but only in the last few years. We recall very well that until about 1938, we would arise before dawn on Christmas morning, take a .38 revolver into the yard, and fire a round into the ground. This was in a city, and my neighbors on every side were doing the same thing.

A standard stocking-stuffer for children was a package or two of firecrackers. They were strung together so you could light the fuse, and all the crackers would pop off in sequence. Most of us, of course, could not afford to be so extravagant. We pulled the little crackers apart and set them off one at a time. They made a very light little pop!

But the odor of this burning powder came to be as Christmasy as the smell of cedar Christmas trees, ginger cookies, and baking turkey.

As we grew older and slightly more affluent, we would

order by mail packages of fireworks that included such sophisticated devices as pinwheels, Roman candles, and even bombs of enormous noise-power. In communities near the South Carolina border, where fireworks are still legally sold, the custom persists to some extent, but in the inland towns like Raleigh, we hear only an occasional blast.

Incidentally, another noise custom seems to be dying out. This was the almost universal blowing of whistles and ringing of bells to herald the entry of a new year. Exactly at midnight on December 31, all the steam whistles in a town — the factory, the sawmill, the locomotives — would cut loose. They were joined by the pealing of church bells. In a town like Greensboro or Winston-Salem, with dozens of factories, the din was delightful to youngsters privileged to stay up that long. Factories with no night shifts would arrange to have a whistle-cord-puller on hand, and churches managed to have someone ready at the bell rope.

You still hear some of this, but nothing like it was 25 years ago, when a town was fairly rocked by a variety of whistles and bells — some shrill, some deep, some raucous, some melodious.

— *Previously published in* The State, *March 15, 1968.*

Christmas
in the Early Piedmont

*"We will send for some of our loving Neighbors and be merry
altogether. We shall lay aples in the fire to roast, tell thee a merry
tale, and sing the melodious Carols of several pleasant tunes; and
we'l be higly pigly one with another."*

Our piedmont Christmas of the late 18th century
centered around the German settlers who celebrated the
seasons with religious observances and social
gatherings. The approach of winter brought a slower pace to
backcountry farm life with leisure time for enjoying the
company of friends and relatives in worship and play. Several
smaller groups of local settlers added the customs of their
homelands to Christmas here on the frontier, including the
English, the Welsh, and the French.

The Scots-Irish Presbyterians were slow to abandon their
Puritanism, however. This group of settlers believed Christmas
should be treated no differently than any other day, condemning
both religious and social festivities. Many years passed before the
Scots-Irish began joining their neighbors in celebrating Christmas.

— *Previously published in* The State, *December 1985.*

A Simple Meal

By Wanda Duncan

Here's a recipe for a feast, abundant with holiday cheer and special memories: Bring together people who care about one another and who cherish tradition. Add the flavors of warm coffee and a lightly sweetened bun. Mingle with aromas of beeswax and fragrant greenery. Blend in seasonal music, twinkling candlelight, a special holiday message, and a beautiful, softly lit star. Serve generously with love at Christmastime.

A Moravian-style love feast is one of the most sensory-rich experiences of the Christmas season. While originally brought to North Carolina by the Moravians in the 1700s, love feasts have since been adopted and embraced by other denominations and are celebrated every year in North Carolina from the mountains to the coast.

The love feast's beginnings trace back to an ancient practice — the agape meal described in the New Testament and shared by members of the early Christian church. Revived in Herrnhut, Germany, by the Moravian Church in 1727, it was then and is today a meaningful way to signify harmony and love, shared by a community of believers. The love feast is a beloved tradition of incorporating a simple meal into worship. Moravian churches hold love feasts every Christmas as well as for other special occasions throughout the year.

MORAVIAN TRADITION

The first love feast in North Carolina was held in November 1753 at what is now the historic settlement of Bethabara in Forsyth County. A band of 15 Moravian men had made their way down the Shenandoah Valley into North Carolina from Bethlehem, Pennsylvania. Their destination was the Wachovia Tract, sold to the Moravians by the Earl of Granville in England. The weary travelers celebrated their arrival at Bethabara with a love feast; their "feast" was likely pumpkin mush, and they recorded in their diary that while they ate, "the wolves and the panthers howled and screamed in the forests near by."

They sang a hymn composed especially for the occasion:

We hold arrival love feast here in Carolina land,
A company of Brethren true, a little pilgrim band.
Called by the Lord to be of those
Who through the whole wide world do go,
To bear Him witness everywhere,
And naught but Jesus know.

Modern-day Moravian-style Christmas love feasts include some unique customs that distinguish them from candlelight Christmas Eve services of other denominations. The simple meal shared at a love feast usually consists of a bun flavored slightly with spices and citrus, accompanied by a mug of sweetened, cream-laden coffee. Tea, hot chocolate, or hot cider might be substituted for the coffee.

Dieners (female servers) and sacristans (male servers) distribute the buns, coffee, and candles in an orderly manner. In some congregations, worshipers leave their seats to share pieces of their bread with others nearby.

While worshipers enjoy their feast, choirs and other musical ensembles perform Christmas selections. The thousands of North Carolinians who enjoy love feasts these days don't hear wolves and panthers. More likely, they are serenaded with angelic voices of adult and children's choirs, hymn tunes played by brass bands, ringing of bright handbells, and heartfelt congregational singing.

The minister reads the Christmas story from the Gospel of Luke and brings a Christmas message.

For many who attend the Moravian Christmas love feast, their favorite part is the singing of the Moravian Christmas carol, "Morning Star." As the lights dim in the sanctuary, one small child leads the singing, and the congregation echoes the verse: "Morning Star, O cheering sight, ere thou cam'st, how dark Earth's night."

The candles, brought out by the dieners and sacristans at the conclusion of the service, are usually made from golden beeswax, with a red ruffled crepe-paper trim at the base of each candle. Most Moravian churches today distribute candles to everyone in attendance; some hand out the candles already lit, while others allow the flame to pass, neighbor to neighbor, along the pews. The closing carol may be "Morning Star" or some other favorite, and everyone holds his or her candle high during the singing of the last stanza.

A SERVICE SHARED

It is less than two miles as a crow could fly on a frosty December night between the historic Bethabara settlement and Wait Chapel on the campus of Wake Forest University. The Chapel has been celebrating the Moravian love feast since the 1960s. Begun by Moravian students at Wake Forest University, the first service drew fewer than 200 people; now, with more than 2,000 in attendance each year, this non-Moravian sanctuary holds what has become the largest Christmas love feast in the world.

Nearly 150 miles west, at First Presbyterian of Asheville, a Moravian Christmas love feast has been held every year since 1999. With the help of former Moravians in the congregation, the youth of the church organize and lead a love feast service on a Wednesday night in December. The young people take the opportunity during the service to explain the different Moravian customs: 18th-century Moravian outfits, the 26-pointed paper star, dieners and sacristans, buns, coffee, and trimmed candles. "Morning Star" is sung responsively between a child and the congregation.

John Wesley, the founder of the Methodist denomination, encountered the Moravians in Savannah in 1737; he observed the love feast service and brought it into the Methodist tradition. Methodists regularly held love feasts throughout the late 1700s and into the mid-1800s. Although love feasts are no longer a standard service in the Methodist church, there are many Methodist congregations statewide that celebrate the Christmas season with a love feast, Moravian style.

Regardless of the setting, whether Moravian or not, the Christmas love feast is a favorite tradition across the state of North Carolina. This unique celebration with Germanic roots has endured and spread from Bethabara to Belmont, Winston-Salem to Williamston, Gastonia to Goldston, Franklin to Fayetteville. Students from Elon to Queens to Wake Forest universities serve as hosts for love feasts on their campuses. Baptists, Methodists, Presbyterians, and Lutherans join Moravians in sharing a simple meal in their sanctuaries every December, re-creating the recipe for a one-of-a-kind holiday feast.

— *Previously published in* Our State, *December 2005.*

CHAPTER 3

Recipes

Secrets for making favorite foods have been
passed along from one generation to the next —
including these time-proven holiday treats.

James K. Polk Christmas Fruit Cake

1 pound butter
12 eggs
1 teaspoon cloves
1 teaspoon each powdered allspice, mace, and nutmeg
1 pound sugar
1 pound flour (after browned and sifted)
1 tablespoon cinnamon
3 pounds seeded raisins
1 pound citron
^{1}/$_2$ pound blanched almonds
juice of 3 large oranges
1 pound candied pineapple
1 pound currants
^{1}/$_2$ pound pecans
1 pint wine or substitute
1 pound dates

Chop almonds, and stir into the orange juice. Mix batter thoroughly, and using hands, begin adding the fruit, a little of each kind at a time. When very stiff, add orange juice and the wine or [its] substitute.

Bake in one large pan with a stem or in several small ones. Line bottom and sides of pan with strips of brown wrapping paper. Grease the pan with lard, and paper well; pour in the batter. Allow 2 inches of space from the rim for rising.

Preheat the oven to 150°, and set a small pan of water inside to keep the cake from drying too much. After the cake has baked for half an hour, turn it once. Continue baking. When the cake stops singing and the testing straw comes out clean, remove it from oven at once. The cake will weigh a full 16 pounds and should take 6½ hours to bake.

Allow it to cool in the pan. Smaller cakes cooked together in the oven take from 3 to 4 hours, depending on size and number.

By Evelyn Polk Norton, Old North State Cook Book, *December 17, 1949. Evelyn Polk Norton was a great-granddaughter of Marshall Polk, the brother of President James K. Polk.*

— *Previously published in* The State, *December 1988.*

Moravian Cookies

Right after Thanksgiving is over is the time to start getting ready to make "Christmas Cakes," if you live in Salem. "Christmas Cakes" (Moravian cookies) mean only one thing — the little paper-thin cakes cut in every conceivable shape and pattern: stars, crescents, leaves, animals, birds, little men and women. Of course, there are other cakes of all kinds made before Christmas by all good housekeepers — layer cakes, loaf cakes, fruit cakes, — but they are not "Christmas Cakes." Those are something special!

Making "Christmas Cakes" is something not to be entered into lightly. It is an important occasion. No outside engagements whatsoever can be sandwiched in during the baking time. When you bake "Christmas Cakes," you bake them and do nothing else for the time being.

These cookies can be bought, but half the fun of them is baking them in your own kitchen and having your whole house and even your neighborhood perfumed with their fragrance, which is like nothing else on earth.

To be good, the dough for these cakes has to be rolled to exactly the thinness of paper — say wrapping paper, no thicker. Then it has to be cut into innumerable patterns. The handling of these cakes from dough-board to baking-tin is an art in itself. And when they are in the oven baking, they can and will burn in the twinkling of an eye.

This recipe is another of those old recipes that has been handed down for generations and used year after year. To make "Christmas Cakes" you have to have, first, the patience of Job, then a calm and tranquil disposition (not easily flustered), good judgment, and above all else, the trait of "stick-to-it-iveness." Don't let all this discourage you: You may make a big success of your "Christmas Cake" baking, and if you do, you are to be congratulated, for you really have accomplished something.

— *Excerpted from* The State, *December 10, 1960.*

"CHRISTMAS CAKES"

1 quart best New Orleans black molasses
3/4 pounds lard and butter mixed
3/4 pounds brown sugar
2 heaping teaspoons [baking] soda
1/2 cup boiling water
1 ounce ginger
1 ounce cinnamon
1 ounce cloves
flour enough to make a rather stiff dough

Mix molasses and lard after having first warmed them to a lukewarm temperature in separate vessels. Then add sugar, gradually beating the mixture all the time. Put [baking] soda into half cup of boiling water, and stir into mixture. Mix the spices with some of the flour and stir in. Then add enough flour, very gradually, to make a dough about the consistency of bread dough. Let this dough stand in a cool place for at least 24 hours to season before beginning to bake your cakes.

Editor's Note: The recipe from 1960 ends here, but similar recipes in *The Carol Dare Cookbook* (1971) add: Roll very thin on floured board. Cut in shapes with cookie cutters, and bake on greased tins at 350°, watching the cookies to take them out as soon as they are brown.

Seafoam

*"An older cousin ... always made seafoam candy for Granny.
I thought it was absolutely the best candy ever,
even better than fudge."*

2 cups brown sugar
$^1/_2$ cup water
1 egg white
1 teaspoon vanilla
$^1/_2$ cup chopped nuts

Combine brown sugar and water, and boil until soft ball or
239° on candy thermometer. Beat egg white until very stiff;
[continue beating while adding] sugar syrup slowly and lightly
to egg white. Put in vanilla and chopped nuts. Drop by
spoonfuls on waxed paper.

— *From Martha Long. Previously published in* Our State, *December 2000.*

Hatteras Cake

"[One Christmas dinner favorite] we called Poor Man's Cake.
Missing some ingredients usually expected and full of raisins,
it may have been a substitute for fruitcake."

Sift together: 4 cups flour, 1 tablespoon baking powder,
1 tablespoon baking soda, 2 teaspoons nutmeg, and 2 teaspoons
cinnamon.

Cook one package raisins [5-10 oz.] in enough water to cover.
Save juice [to add as needed to moisten] batter. Puree cooked
raisins, add 1 cup shortening, 2 cups sugar, and 1 teaspoon salt.
[Add dry ingredients,] mix all together, and bake at 300° in a
greased pan of suitable size for 50-60 minutes. [Allow cake to
cool in pan.]

Mix together ½ package of confectioners' sugar, butter, and
additional cinnamon, to taste.

— *Previously published in* Our State, *December 2000.*

Hatteras Island Pone Bread

"We were fortunate to have a goose as the main attraction at Christmas dinner ... and the usual pies and cakes. Pone bread, a heavy bread made with meal and molasses and soured before baking, was very popular in some homes."

5 cups white corn meal
3 tablespoons molasses
4 cups hot water
6 tablespoons sugar
1 1/2 teaspoons salt
1 cup cold water
1 cup sifted flour
2 tablespoons shortening

Put meal and molasses in bowl, add hot water, and stir well. Add sugar, salt, and cold water. Add flour, and mix well. Cover for a few hours, or overnight. Melt shortening in 2-quart pan, pour in mixture, and bake covered at 350° for 1-1 1/2 hours [until a toothpick inserted in the center comes out clean].

Let stand until cool. Cut in squares like corn bread.

— *Previously published in* Our State, *December 2000.*

Made for Christmas

Sausage was made for it.
Turkeys were kept for it.
Potato custards were baked for it.
Dried peach and apple tarts were packed in columns for it.
Hominy was beaten for it.
Locust and persimmon beer were prepared for it.
Possums were fattened for it.
The last of the winter apples were guarded for it.
Tallow candles were molded for it.
The great woodpile was heaped for it.
Often, also, eggs and whisky and brown sugar
were procured for the eggnog and stored away for it.

— North Carolina Chronicle, *Raleigh, December 1892.*

Savoring the Delights of Christmases Past

By Carol Dare

What would Christmas be without the special aromas and tastes that evoke memories of holidays past?

The holidays are a time when many cooks dig out the recipes for old favorites like Christmas cookies, wassail bowls, Moravian cakes, and a host of other special treats.

Over the years, *The State* has no doubt contributed to the holiday recipe collections of many people. As reprinted in *The Carol Dare Cookbook*, here are [three] recipes from Christmases past for young cooks who want to widen their repertoires or more experienced cooks seeking to recall a special holiday from the past.

Merry Christmas!

— Previously published in The State, *December 1987.*

CHRISTMAS COOKIES

These shortbread-type cookies are wonderful without icing
for dunking in coffee or hot chocolate. With icing and candies,
they make a sweet treat.

1 cup butter
2 cups sugar
4 eggs
1 cup milk
$^1/_2$ teaspoon salt
3 teaspoons baking powder
6 cups flour

Cream the butter. Add sugar gradually. Add the eggs, and beat thoroughly. Mix salt and baking powder with the flour. Add the liquid and dry ingredients alternately to the egg mixture, adding the dry ingredients first and last. Mix thoroughly.

Chill dough overnight. In the morning, roll thin on a floured board. Cut into various shapes with cookie cutters. Bake on greased baking sheets 10 minutes in a moderately hot oven [about 350°-375°]. Cool. Ice with confectioners' sugar and milk icing. Decorate with colored sugars and candies.

— from December 20, 1947

WASSAIL BOWL

"Here we come a-wassailing among the leaves so green /
Here we come a-wand'ring so fair to be seen /
Love and joy come to you and to you your wassail, too /
And God bless you and send you a happy New Year /
And God send you a happy New Year."

4 quarts cider
³/4 cup sugar
1 cup brown sugar
2 tablespoons stick cinnamon, crushed
¹/₂ cup orange juice
¹/₂ cup lemon juice
16 whole cloves
¹/₂ teaspoon salt

Simmer all ingredients for 10 minutes. Strain and reheat when ready to serve. A nice effect is achieved by floating little red apples in punch bowl.

— from December 20, 1947

MORAVIAN CHRISTMAS TREE CAKES
*"The little Christmas cakes, cut in shapes, that adorn
all Moravian Christmas trees, are made by mothers
and grandmothers at home."*

1 pint [2 cups] molasses
$^1/_2$ pound [2 cups] brown sugar
$^1/_2$ pound [2 sticks] butter
1 quart [4 cups] flour, or more if needed
1 tablespoon each:
    allspice
    ginger
    cinnamon
    cloves
1 tablespoon soda dissolved in water

Melt molasses, sugar, and butter in a bowl on a warm stove,
and stir well. Pour into flour and spices, and add soda. Knead to
smoothness. Let stand 24 hours. Roll paper-thin, cut in shapes,
bake in moderately hot oven (about 450°) until brown [about
2-3 minutes].

— *from Adelaide Fries, Winston-Salem, December 9, 1950*

From the *Wilson Mirror*, December 1889:
Sage advice for a cook can't go far beyond turkey stuffing.

❖

From the *Greensboro Daily News*,
December 26, 1915:
The hour changes; the dish doesn't.
1 p.m. — Stuffed turkey.
2 p.m. — Stuffed, turkey.

❖

From the *Henderson Gold Leaf*, December 1887:
The Editor's Christmas turkey has not come yet, and
indications are that we will have to put up with a common
barnyard rooster — if we can get a rooster.

❖

From the *Charlotte News*, December 1932:
Christmas comes but once a year
For which we're truly grateful.
Turkey is a glorious dish,
But turkey hash is hateful.

Christmas Possum

Jesse Bullock, the champion fox hunter and game chicken raiser in this section, has eight possums "big (he says) as a month-old pig." He will share these at Christmas and requests us to invite his friends to cross their legs under his mahogany on that day.

— Tarboro Southerner, *December 17, 1875.*

Better Late than Never

Miss Alma Holland got a 100-pound sack of cotton seed meal as a Christmas gift for Mrs. Charles S. Mangum. Every once in a while, for weeks, she would take it to the Mangum house, but no one was at home strong enough to lift it. So she would drive away with it and hope for better luck next time.

The sack was carried through the village nobody knows how many times. At last, it was delivered — on the 26th of February.

— *From the* Chapel Hill Weekly, *February 28, 1936.*

CHAPTER 4

Memories

Christmases past pile up in our minds like treasured
gifts to be taken out and enjoyed again and again.

Popcorn Tree Christmas

By Anna-Lisa Fales

My father had just transported us all to the country, and the rambling old house felt cold and empty compared to our city flat. Mama threw blankets over packing boxes to fill corners, but it didn't help. When Papa got a fire roaring in the pot-bellied stove that dominated the parlor, we sat watching the light wink from its isinglass windows. It was depressing.

Suddenly, Mama jumped up. "This house needs a Christmas tree!" My brother went into the nearby woods with Papa to cut a tall, perfect tree.

The whole house was soon redolent with spruce, but Mama was in tears. "The Christmas box!" she cried. "The movers must have lost it."

It hardly seemed worthwhile, but Papa and my brother anchored the tree in a rough wooden base. At lunch, we ate with long faces until Mama said, "Hurry up, girls. I need your help."

That day we baked about 100 spice cookies in animal shapes. The honor of pushing holes in them with a knitting needle before they cooled was given to me. Frosted in white and strung with red strings, they made glistening ornaments.

The rest of the day was a happy frenzy of apple polishing, cranberry stringing, and popcorn popping. Christmas Eve morning, Papa was waiting to instruct us beside the round oak table, spread with white paper. We'd never heard of origami, but we practiced the ancient Japanese art until we'd made 50 three-dimensional stars. Papa made a large perfect one to grace the top of the tree, while we knotted green strings around the stems of tiny red apples.

My sister, always the bossy one, told me where to place them on lower branches. She, being taller, decorated upper branches, alternating loops of plump popcorn with red cranberry ropes. Last of all, she placed the stars. I would never have told her, but the effect was artistic. When all was in place except Papa's special star, I felt his eyes on me.

"I wonder," he teased, "who would like to put this on?"

Suddenly I was on my brother's shoulders, the wonderful star in my hands. Trembling with excitement, I placed it carefully over the topmost twig. "I'm glad the movers lost the ornaments!" I said.

I don't recall what my presents were that year, but I shall always remember how I stole alone into the chilly parlor where our tree presided like a lovely queen. It was just before we all gathered there to exchange gifts.

The parlor smelled of spruce and candle-wax, spice cookies, and apples. Mama's candleholders from Sweden stood on either side of the room, casting a soft glow. Cranberries became rubies, popcorn was carved ivory, cookies and paper stars sparkled against the green.

And sparkling among my memories, a perennial gift, is that first Christmas in the country, when the popcorn tree made magic in our home.

— *Previously published in* The State, *December 1985.*

Oh, Horrors!

Christmas is coming, and were it not for the noise and confusion ... and the firecrackers, and all the other unnamed horrors and abominations, we should be much inclined to rejoice therein. But whether we rejoice or not, the eggnog stock begins to look up. By the by, eggnog is a most villainous compound to get sober on.

— Wilmington Daily Journal, *December 23, 1851.*

Father and
the Christmas Mints

BY RUTH MOOSE

In mid-December, when the nights became clear, sharp and cold, my father whistled home with a brown bulky package under his arm. Robbie, my younger brother, and I knew the time had come. Tonight we'd make mints.

We hung over the table as Daddy unwrapped his package until out rolled fat bags of sugar, squares of real butter, and a small drugstore bottle of magic.

After supper, Mama hung up her apron and tucked a clean white dishtowel around Daddy's waist. He held up his arms, turned on his toes as she fitted it, then left. We giggled, then rushed to get out the special pan, thermometer, wooden spoon, shears, and waxed paper. From the top shelf in the dark of the cool, floury-smelling pantry, we stood on a stool to reach the tins — we wanted them down and ready. From its place between the refrigerator and the wall, we pulled out the black-swirled marble slab. Daddy said it weighed a ton and lifted it to the table.

I measured sugar; Robbie lit the gas, getting to blow out the match and be asked where the flame went. Daddy cut butter, his hand flat on the knife and the blocks of butter falling like pale dominos. These went atop the sugar evenly sprinkled; then water went over it all. Lastly, the thermometer was poked in upright as a warning.

The pot bubbled and in the sugar-sweetened air, we sang like drunken bees, working and deliciously waiting.

When Daddy took the thermometer out, pronounced it done, we stood back as he poured out the crystal puddle, watching it spread. The edges rolled out, scalloped and thin, then stopped, safe within our buttered space.

We leaned over the lake, and Daddy, elbows out and with a small bottle in his hands, unloosed the cap. Oil of peppermint wafted into the room, so strong, I expected it to take a shape and ask our command.

The milky edges of the candy were lifted, fluted all around like a huge pie shell as it cooled. And we all buttered our twice-clean hands. Daddy stretched the hank of candy rope, looped it and brought it back again. It's all in the wrist, he said, twisting, looping, snapping. And we tried. The warm candy was heavy in our hands like something alive, bent on escaping. He took it back and stretched it in, around, and over, slick and shiny. He pulled faster, harder. Robbie and I stretched waxed paper atop the freezer, the washer, tray table, even the seat of an extra chair. Daddy patted the ribbed snake out and snipped it to bits. Rows of rectangular buttons. The word was cream. Now, they have to cream, he said, and we went to bed sleepy eyed and full of secrets.

Each day Robbie and I tested. One each, "to see if they're creamed yet." And four days later they were — mints like bites of winter clouds all ice and soft, cool down the backs of our throats, lingering on our tongues.

HOMEMADE GIFTS

We put them into the tins and pretty bottles and jars. They

shone like jewels topped with bows and cards.

Like prizes, we carried them to school. Merry Christmas to our teachers, the principal at her clean desk, Willie in the furnace room, Bernice and Velma, starched and white in the cafeteria. Nobody was supposed to "buy gifts" for their teachers, but nobody said you couldn't make one. The teacher's desk was littered with small packages, surrounded by whispers. What did you bring? Earrings, a billfold, handkerchiefs, gloves. I was relieved. No one else brought mints.

At lunch, Miss Martin called me aside. "Did your mother make these?" she said holding the half-empty jar.

"No," I said, "my father."

"Oh." She held my shoulders and looked at me again. "They're really good. Tell her how much I liked them."

"But ..." and I stopped. It wasn't polite to correct a teacher. Later I heard her in the hall, sharing with the 5th grade teacher next door. "Aren't they marvelous? Ruth's mother made them."

That night I told Daddy. He laughed. Last year's teacher had said the same thing. Robbie said his teacher said "your mother," too. We reached our warm hands into the round tin, smiled, shared the last of the leftover mints and crumbs ... and a secret.

— *Previously published in* The State, *December 1978.*

A Discriminating Church-goer

Reverend Patton, a Presbyterian minister of Raleigh, described one of his members as a "C.E. member."

Someone asked, "Christian Endeavor?"

"No," the minister replied. "Christmas and Easter. They're the only two occasions you'll find him attending church."

— *Previously published in* The State, *February 15, 1941.*

The Most Memorable Hallelujah Chorus

By Katherine G. Rogers

B ack when barbershop quartets were as popular as hard
cider and plug tobacco, nobody invited my father,
Murray Grantham, to join a new group of singers. After
all, even his whistling was wheezy.

"Just the same," he liked to say, "nobody enjoys music more'n
I do, or remembers the tunes and words better. And I can really
hum!" To prove it, he would hum "Rock of Ages."

A birthright Quaker, he was always moved by lofty hymns,
but it wasn't until the Christmas of 1912 that he heard religious
music excelling all he had known before. It made him feel
exultant.

By then he was a middle-aged but genial Greensboro grocer
with a wife and four children, including me. We lived in a
clapboard house only two blocks from the State Normal and
Industrial College for Women (now the University of North
Carolina at Greensboro), and his grocery store was just across
the yard from our house.

Scanning the *Greensboro Daily News* the day after
Thanksgiving while humming "What a Friend We Have in

Jesus," Papa was struck by the headline, "Christmas at the Normal." The accompanying article elated him:

Dr. Wade R. Brown, dean of music at the college, will conduct Handel's great Christian oratorio, the 'Messiah,' December 15 in the auditorium of Students' Building. Distinguished soloists will be imported from New York City, but the chorus will consist of musically-talented college students.

"This presentation of the great work will be the first in Greensboro and even in the entire Piedmont area," Dr. Brown explained. "In creating this oratorio, the composer, Frideric Handel, selected divinely-inspired passages from Isaiah and the New Testament, and voiced them anew in his divinely-inspired melodies and harmonies."

Papa didn't read the article to us at supper, but he told us about it. "Just imagine!" he exclaimed. "Hearing in all those heavenly melodies the Bible verses I've long known by heart — especially the glorious prophecy of Isaiah, 'For unto us a child is born.'"

Would I get to hear that joyous song? After kissing me goodnight, Papa promised to take me.

During the next two weeks, his business with the college students tapered off. Women from the Normal College usually came during their afternoon Walking Period — the only time the strict Lady Principal let them go even two blocks from the campus without chaperones. Now, they stayed away to practice for the "Messiah." I missed them, for I had often waited on them at the candy showcase when I came straight to the store from my third-grade room at the Normal's Practice School. (The older students practiced teaching there.) Although I was just eight years old, I was allowed to help Papa because at last I could see over the counter.

Our regular customers, including Normal College teachers, kept marveling about the oratorio and said they certainly wouldn't miss it. At that time, the Normal was still small enough to be neighborly. Folks living near the campus flocked there for free entertainment, including concerts, plays, hockey games, and commencement exercises.

The night before the oratorio, I was so excited that I slept only in snatches and dreamt of angels, flocks of sheep, and the wondrous sound of golden harps. As the snow began to fall before breakfast, Mama quoted an old saying: "Snow in the morning's like an old woman's dance — soon ended." But big flakes continued to swirl till dinnertime. That evening, to make sure Papa and I would get to the "Messiah" on time, Mama called us to supper early. It was mostly leftovers from the big dinner at noon but had an added Christmas surprise: syllabub. My big sister had already eaten and was minding the store.

After supper, I waited in the sitting room while Papa put on his Sunday clothes. I was already dolled up in my new blue and pink Alamance-plaid dress. My red Sunday coat was waiting on the horsehair lounge, along with a red knitted jacket and matching stocking cap and mittens. I was happy and thankful for all the sewing and knitting Mama had done for my Christmas gifts.

Still waiting for Papa, I put on my black rubbers with heavy soles and funny tongues curving over the insteps. Pretty soon I had to move away from the blazing log in the fireplace because my long winter underwear was getting so hot and bothersome. I hated it, anyway, especially having to fold the stretchy fabric into humps behind my calves before I could pull on my black cotton stockings.

When Papa came in, handsome in his gray Sunday suit and smelling of bay rum, he held his overcoat looped over one arm and his black derby in the other hand. Mama took one look.

"Murray," she said, "you are going among refined and elegant people. That black velvet collar on our overcoat looks elegant. But your pants legs all stuffed in your boots do not. Besides, it's mild enough weather to leave the legs out, wide and free."

"Reckon so, Omelia." He jerked the pants legs free.

"Another thing — it could turn nippy on your ears under that derby." Handing him the new black and white scarf she had knitted, she said, "Merry Christmas." He pulled her close and kissed her.

Outside, the moon shone on Mama's prize tulip tree — a full moon, golden and wondrous. Some of our neighbors waved to us from the brick sidewalk. They, too, were headed for the Normal, Papa surmised. After quickly walking the two blocks to campus, we climbed the front steps to the lobby.

As we hurried toward the circular stairway to the auditorium, I barely glanced at the massive bronze statue of Minerva, Roman goddess of wisdom, which I had often seen as a model for Normal students. We climbed the stairs to the main entrance of the auditorium, where a tall college girl stood in the open doorway. Red-haired, she wore a flowing white dress with an immense, yellow silk rose at her shoulder.

She was one of Papa's most faithful Normal customers, and — as with all his customers — he always greeted her by name. I often had sold her chocolate-covered cherries. "Good evening, Miss Eunice," he said, "and congratulations on your elegant yellow regalia."

"Thank you, Mr. Grantham."

"Your rose — it's a sign, I take it, that you are now the chief usher."

"Yes, it's an honor. But it's also a responsibility, one that obliges me right now to tell you I can't admit your little girl to the oratorio. Dr. Brown has ruled that no child under 12 years old can be admitted."

"Under 12?" Papa was unbelieving and indignant. "My little

girl, though only 8, behaves better than many grownups. And besides, she loves music and will listen attentively and joyously."

"I'm sorry, Mr. Grantham. It's not a question of your little daughter's behavior or appreciation of music. There simply isn't a seat for her or any child under 12. The concert has attracted greater public interest than was anticipated, and the space is limited. So when Dr. Brown realized how great the attendance would be, he ruled out children under 12."

Reluctantly, Papa took my arm and led me back down the circular stairway, muttering as we went, "Looks like Wade Brown could have warned me. He was in the store just a week ago to pay his grocery bill." By then, we almost bumped into the statue of Minerva. Suddenly, with his hand on her mighty arm he said, "You know it, you Pagan Goddess of Wisdom. Solomon knew it. William Penn the great American Quaker, knew it, and I know it: Where there's a will, there's a way, providing there's also common sense." He turned to me. "Well, honeybunch, I see the way now to best Wade Brown and his rule against you."

Following him out of the lobby, I pulled on my mittens. He sat down on the top step and crammed his loose pants legs into his boots. Grinning when he got up, he slipped me a horehound drop, then led me to the moonlit path that wound behind the Students' Building. He kept kicking at little snowdrifts — why I didn't know. Then, suddenly, he stooped and yanked out a snow-fringed pine branch that had blown off a tree. "Strong and just the right length," he said, puzzling me.

We stepped onto the snow-covered fire escape that led to the back door of the auditorium. Papa used the pine branch to scrape the snow from the two bottom steps. "I'll keep scraping," he said, "so we can safely climb to the top. That is, I'll reach up from one step to the one above, clear it, climb up, then reach up to the next, clear it and so on. You will follow me, honeybunch, hanging on to my coattails."

Finally, we reached the moon-lit landing at the top, and Papa again scraped the snow off. Looking through the glass door at the back of the auditorium, we saw that the seats were almost filled. On the stage, the chorus of Normal girls was assembling. The glass door was partly ajar, and we could hear the orchestra tuning up.

Papa propped himself against the back railing, opened his overcoat, and pulled my shoulders back against his chest. Then he buttoned me inside the coat, leaving a gap for only my eyes, nose and mouth. "This way," he said, "you'll keep snug and warm."

Just then came a burst of applause. The soloists entered the stage with Dr. Brown, and they all bowed. Lifting his baton, Dr. Brown prompted the orchestra to begin, and from the first majestic strains of "Comfort Ye" to the final "Amen," Papa and I stood entranced.

The oratorio had three parts. During the brief intermissions, we told each other how the fabulous singing had carried us away. Papa was moved to tears, as expected, by Isaiah's prophecy set to music: "For unto us a child is born ... and his name shall be called Wonderful, Counselor ... the Everlasting Father, the Prince of Peace." I was dazzled by "O Thou That Tellest Good Tidings" and "Every Valley Shall Be Exalted."

But we both were ecstatic over the "Hallelujah Chorus," with its grandeur, repeated hallelujahs, and the pledge "forever, forever!" Papa, echoing those sentiments, said the beauty and promise of those Christmas hallelujahs would live in his mind and heart forever.

— *Previously published in* The State, *December 1988.*

Putting the Tree
Where It Belongs

Grandmother and daughter were planning Christmas. "Where will we put the tree this year? Junior can walk now, you know."

"He climbs, too. How about on the mantle?"

"O Mama, what kind of a tree can you put on the mantle? Why don't we just keep Junior in the playpen until after Christmas?"

"Junior hasn't been in the playpen without protest for two months."

So what did they do? They put the tree in the playpen — presents, too. It worked fine.

— Previously published in The State, *December 14, 1957.*

Champion
Christmas
Shopper

By Closs Peace Harris

Young Robert Stubbs Hight, eight-year-old son of Mr. and Mrs. Blannie Hight of Henderson, pushed his chair back from the breakfast table.

"I'm going downtown today and do some Christmas shopping," he announced to his parents. "It may take me all day, so don't bother to wait dinner for me. I may eat downtown."

"Have you got any money, son?" asked his father. "If you haven't, I'll let you have some."

"No, thank you," said Robert. "I have my own money."

"How much have you got?" asked his father, curiously.

"Eighty cents," he proudly replied. "I've been saving up for Christmas for some time."

And so, armed with his 80 cents, Master Hight went shopping.

Dinner hour arrived, but no Robert. His mother began to wonder what had become of him.

Shortly before 2 o'clock, she happened to be looking out

through the front window and saw a taxicab drive into the yard. She saw that her son was seated on the rear seat. Fearing that an accident had happened to him, she rushed out on the front porch.

"Anything the matter, Robert?" she cried.

"Not a thing," he exclaimed, as he got out and paid the driver.

His arms were full of bundles. A little questioning on the part of his mother revealed the fact that he had purchased seven different Christmas presents; had had four hot dogs, one ice cream cone, and a Coca-Cola for lunch; and had paid his taxi fare home.

If you know of anyone who did better than that on 80 cents this Christmas, I'd appreciate it if you would let me know about it.

— *Previously published in* The State, *December 25, 1937.*

Captain Crunch

BY AMY JO WOOD

My Uncle Olin lived his whole life in the rural countryside of Davidson County, which may have caused some people to label him a simple man.

The youngest of eight children, he got bypassed for much of the hard work on the tobacco farm where he grew up, but as a teenager he served in the U.S. Army during the Korean War. When he returned, he married and had two children, a boy and a girl. They lived about a mile from his original homeplace, so his sisters and brother who had moved away assumed he'd take care of their widowed mom and unmarried aunt. Which he did, without complaint. He mowed the women's lawn during the summers, chopped logs in winter for their wood stove, and took them to town whenever they needed to go to the doctor, the grocery store, or to pay a light bill.

The Olin I knew smoked More cigarettes and fixed old cars when everyone else had given up on the clunkers. He drank lots of instant coffee and liked to talk politics on Sunday afternoons in the kitchen of his mother's house — a place where she displayed ceramic frogs on the window sill and stored toothpicks in their mouths, covered the table with a plastic cloth, and nailed a calendar from the local funeral parlor on the wood walls to keep up with the passing of time.

The kitchen was a gathering spot of sorts for generations. Despite a relative's age, interest, and geographic locale, everyone eventually came back home on Sunday afternoons to eat homemade fried apple pies, persimmon pudding, or fresh-from-the-garden watermelon.

Olin moved back to the two-story farmhouse once he got divorced. Everybody assumed it was temporary, and I never thought to inquire about the man's hopes and dreams.

WASTE NOT, WANT NOT

My red-headed uncle went on with his life and eventually created two new Christmas traditions despite his bachelor existence: gifts of carved animal figurines, which he handcrafted in the wood shop where he worked, and bags of Trash Snack Mix, a glorious combination of cereal, cashews, peanuts, and pretzels.

For years, family members brought him coupons from newspapers and magazines in October for the various ingredients he would blend into his famous Trash Snack Mix come December. Every Sunday afternoon during the holiday season, visiting sisters, nephews, nieces, children, and grandchildren critiqued Olin's Trash Snack Mix masterpiece for that year.

"Too salty," said some.

"Never could stand pretzels," mused another.

"Generic cereal is as good as Chex," offered others.

"I'm on a diet," a few always replied.

But no one ever refused second helpings.

I loved the Trash Snack Mix more than I loved cheese balls, and I adored cheese balls. For a few years, I thought I was too busy to make it to the country during December, but Olin always filled an old bread sack full of Trash Snack Mix and sent it home with Mom to give to me.

I tried to make sure I sent back words of thanks, but

second-hand appreciation never makes up for a lazy hour of talking about nothing in the kitchen where your grandma raised the children who raised you.

After Olin died, I made it a point to visit the farmhouse every Christmas, but without the Trash Snack Mix to crunch and critique, the afternoons were unbearably quiet.

I miss Uncle Olin.

— Previously published in Our State, *December 2000.*

Christmas Tree Night

By Elizabeth Silance

O n Sunday night before Christmas, we would gather on the crude wooden benches for our Christmas Tree at the church. That's what our little country congregation called it, for we were not sophisticated enough in those days for formal candlelight services. We simply had our Christmas Tree Night.

Never to be really forgotten was the fervent excitement, the oohs and ahhs over the stately beauty of a giant cedar or fragrant pine taken from the woods of a friend. All decked out in borrowed ornaments and paper garlands, it stood in splendor, enveloping all who entered in its special magic.

Gifts were tied to the sturdiest boughs, and others were heaped around the trunk. Small eyes kept straying to the beribboned packages, scarcely able to wait through the ritual that must be followed.

First must come the Carol Sing. If there happened to be present a Sister who could play the piano and would own up to it, the rinky-tink tones of the upright would add to the merriment. If not, everybody just sang out a little louder.

Afterwards, the preacher would get up and read the Christmas story from the book of Luke, and then the Children's Sunday School would march up front and present their program.

Despite nervous giggles and sudden urges of nature, each would recite a poem or sing before the beaming smiles of proud parents who did not notice that Suzie left out a whole line of her "piece" or that Johnny did not know all the words of "Joy to the World."

They would return to their seats quickly, for the preacher would already be standing beside the tree ready to "call out the names."

Every man, woman, boy, girl, and even tiny baby would have a package to unwrap and a "Christmas pretty" to take home. Later, the brown sacks would be passed out to each child under the age of 16. The tempting fruit demanded to be eaten, but it must be taken home, placed in a bowl on the kitchen table for all to look at and smell for a day or two.

Christmas was the aroma of pine and cedar, apples and oranges in brown paper sacks, the sounds of carols and recitations, the magic of Christmas Tree Night at the church.

Still magic

The tree still stands in the corner of the church, but it is a different church now, fully carpeted with comfortable pews lighted with heavy chandeliers.

The tree itself no longer lends its scent to the magic of the moment for it has not been cut from a neighbor's woods; it has been purchased at the local discount store and will be dismantled after the holiday and put away until next year.

There are no gifts for the children, rather gifts of food for those in need cluster around the skinny trunk of the tree. There will be no fruit and nuts in sacks, only those fruit bowls that will be taken later to shut-in members of the church who don't have that treat as often as the children do these days.

I sit there thinking all this, missing things as they were. But then the Sunday School children — mine among them — march in and straight up to the tree to hang their little handmade ornaments while white lights blink and twinkle among the branches while we sing "O Come, All Ye Faithful."

A little girl turns to "say her piece," another lifts her quivering chin and gives forth with a clear "Away in a Manager," as a bathrobed Joseph and sheet-garbed shepherds stand gazing at the small bundle in the hay.

A small Mary gently tucks the cover around the baby doll, and it is all right now. They feel the magic. The magic of Christmas ... the blessing of the Christ child.

— Previously published in The State, *December 1976.*

A Courthouse with Christmas Spirit

Everybody give Pittsboro a great big hand. They've had the courthouse repainted. The building is now a brilliant red with white trimmings, and the steeple is white with green trimmings. With the addition of a few colored electric lights, it would make a fine-looking community Christmas tree.

— *By Carl Goerch,* The State, *November 10, 1935.*

God and the Ration Board

BY JUDITH H. SETTLE

R ecently, my daughter bought a new bike. She's as proud of
it as she was her first shiny red tricycle.

"There's nothing like the wind sweeping across your face
from the seat of a fast-going bike," she says.

"You're right about that," I call as she swings the kickstand aside
and launches a ride around her condo parking lot.

Her excitement trips my memory back more than two
generations. It's December 1944. I am 9½ years old, and I want a
bicycle more than I ever wanted baby dolls. "Don't get your hopes
up," my mom says. "The ration board may not think we qualify
for a bike."

Mom says I get the defense board, the draft board, and the
ration board mixed up. The ration board controls shoes, sugar, and
electric lights. The defense board has sent my father to the
Portsmouth shipyards, and the draft board has shipped six uncles
overseas. White, gold-fringed, silk banners with red stars hang in
my grandparents' windows, signifying to all who pass that sons are
fighting in the war overseas.

Now Christmas is coming to Erwin, my little textile town, and
the war keeps going on. I miss shopping for presents with my
daddy. I miss playing Santa Claus games with my uncles. I worry
about my daddy and my uncles' safety — and wonder if I'll ever

see them again.

I overheard Mom telling our next-door neighbor that she'll have to take time off from the mill and go before the ration board in Raleigh to show cause why I need a bike. "We live over a mile from the post office and the pharmacy and almost a mile from Judy's school. We need a bicycle for transport, for emergencies," she said.

"Since there's no man at your house, maybe your household will qualify," the neighbor replied.

It puzzles me, having to "qualify." I just want a bike. I know we can't have a car. We can't even have rubber-soled tennis shoes. The big red-white-and-blue posters in the post office proclaim, "All metal and rubber for the war effort."

My grandfather has an old, old Ford coupe with deep dents and long scratches on the black fenders. Chunks of rubber are missing from the running boards. It stays parked in the barn. When I asked him why he didn't get it fixed up, he said: "Judy, have you heard the Ford song on the radio?"

"No, sir."

"Pay attention to these words," he said, and his deep, bass voice in singsong fashion bellowed: "There's a Ford in your future / and a Ford in your past / but the Ford you have now, / you'd better make it last."

I think I understand why a lot of metal and rubber were needed to build a tank, an airplane, even a car. But it wouldn't take much for a war bike!

THE COUNTDOWN CONTINUES

It's two weeks till Christmas and time for us to decorate. Mother strings the tree with colored bulbs, and I set up the miniature papier-maché village on the mantel.

Bike thoughts keep swirling through my mind. I see myself in proud ownership. The bike is sky blue with a tan leather seat. A big wire basket on the handlebars holds my books and softball. I breathe deeply and imagine the wind rushing against my face as I swiftly pedal through the town park, past the black bear's cage and the monkey bars. But Mom's words, "Don't get your hopes up," cloud my daydreaming. It is war time, I remind myself.

My favorite building in the miniature village is the chapel. Its steeple sparkles with silver glitter. Its four tiny windows are paned with bits of yellow, oiled paper. There's just room inside for a single, little electric bulb. "Let's burn it all Christmas Day, Mom."

When she answers, her eyes twinkle. "It'll be our Christmas gift from the ration board."

On Christmas Eve we attend evening church services. Before the benediction, I squeeze in a prayer for a bike and, during the recessional, one for the ration board. Afterward, Mom listens to the late war news over our big floor-model radio. I shake the presents under the tree trying to decide whether one holds the white rabbit-fur mittens from the Montgomery Ward catalog. We hug goodnight. I fall asleep, silently reciting "Twas the Night before Christmas."

"WE QUALIFIED!"

Waking early to an inch-deep white yard, I smell Mom's coffee perking and know that I can have a cup, too, with cream and sugar. I want to run to the tree, but I take extra time putting on my chenille robe and slippers.

Slowly I leave my room and walk toward the living room — afraid of what I won't see. But there, in front of the glittering tree, sits the most beautiful blue bike in all the world.

Running to touch it, forgetting my doubts and the war, I shout, "Mom, oh Mom, we qualified!"

It is my dream come true, never mind the skinny frame and "victory bike" tires.

I believe my prayers have been answered. God granted me my wish, but first He had to speak to the ration board.

— *Previously published in* The State, *December 1990.*

Prayer for Peace

By Gertrude Cook Page

O God, we ask Thee just for Peace,
Upon this Christmas day,
Let war and strife forever cease
And love forever stay.

Let none with blood stained lips — soon sealed,
Cry out Thy name in pain.
Let none on gory battlefields
Die for a cause in vain.

God, let all nations near and far,
At Thy feet kneel and pray,
That all may find Thy guiding star
On this, Christ's natal day.

— Previously published in The State, *December 15, 1939.*

CHAPTER 5

The Way It Used to Be

An Old-Fashioned Christmas

BY BILLY ARTHUR

Christmas is a time for traditions, but not all Tar Heel Christmas traditions have been preserved over the years. In fact, since the late-18th and early-19th centuries, quite a lot has changed about the way we celebrate the holidays.

A little digging turned up some interesting information about early Christmas celebrations in North Carolina. Some of the following customs still are practiced. Others are a bit more unusual.

YULE LOGS

Scandinavian immigrants handed down the custom of the yule log to English-speaking countries. At one time, their ancestors kindled huge fires to their god Thor at the feast of their winter solstice.

North Carolinians trudged to the forest way before Christmas to select the biggest log they could find. Then they took it home and soaked it in water for months to make it burn more slowly.

On Christmas Eve, they threw the log onto the back of the fire. As long as it burned on Christmas Day — even to the last glowing embers — slaves had a holiday. When the fire went out, some families kept the remnants until following year to kindle the new yule log.

Tree Decorations

German settlers brought the concept of a Christmas tree to North Carolina. But in Eastern North Carolina, especially in the state's early days, the holly tree was preferred to the evergreen.

In lieu of modern-day tinsel and ornaments, apples were polished and popcorn strung, and paper was cut in fancy shapes. Candy, sweet gumballs dipped in whitewash, and tiny beeswax candles also were used. Everything was handmade.

Throughout the house, vines of smilax, festoons of cedar, holly wreaths, and mistletoe were hung.

'Christmas Time'

In the mountains, according to the *Asheville Citizen Times* in 1949, there were no Christmas holidays, per se. "Christmas Time," the newspaper said, began "promptly at dusk" on December 24 and ended at dusk the following day.

"It was a night and day of being neighborly," the *Times* continued. Singing, shouting, praying, tale telling, prank playing, giving, and receiving were the order of the day.

In preparation, cords of hickory wood were split to keep the fires roaring. The fires were built at dusk and frequently replenished. Families and guests — mostly neighbors — gathered round and shared food, drinks, stories, and traditions.

They cracked walnuts against the "jamrock" and roasted chestnuts "under the forestick." Sometimes, old barn lofts would be lit up for dancing till the crack of dawn.

Fireworks

Christmas was a time for noise. Since most people couldn't afford fireworks, a good substitute was placing a live hickory coal on a flat rock and pounding it with a sledgehammer or a pole axe. The explosion could be heard far away, and it was harmless.

Lots of gunpowder was used in shooting off muzzle-loading shotguns, rifles, and revolvers. Carbide was exploded in tin cans.

According to J.H. Myrover in *The Charlotte Observer*, January 26, 1908: "The only noise (60 years ago) that saluted the (Fayetteville) ear when awaking to the birthday of the Prince of Peace was the bombardment of the village artillerist, who kept it up with an old anvil from the blacksmith shop until he got out of powder or blew off one of his fingers."

CAROLING

On Christmas Eve night, grown-ups, young people, and children went serenading. They carried along their guns, dish pans, musical instruments — banjos, fiddles, guitars, Jews harps, and "mouth organs" — anything they could find that would make a noise.

They visited every house in the community, called out a greeting, sang a song or two, and went inside to warm up and partake of refreshments. Frequently, the families they visited joined them. When the last house was reached, they had a dance.

CHILDREN'S GIFTS

Children hung their biggest and longest pairs of hand-knit stockings for Santa Claus to fill. Most often, he gave them an orange (a rare treat), an apple, a big stick of peppermint candy, mixed nuts, and sun-dried raisins (the most appreciated). In addition, there would be a toy for the youngest child and clothing for the older children.

During the Civil War years, gift-givers had to rely on their ingenuity. Rag dolls often were made with faces of white cloth and black-button eyes. The eyebrows were drawn in pencil, and cheeks and mouths were colored by pokeberry juice. The hair was fashioned of knit black yarn and raveled to become curly.

Those early toys, however, were as appreciated as the popular ones today.

CHARITY

Judging from editorials and old newspaper articles from the 1840s, people then — as now — became more interested in the care of the unfortunate around Christmastime.

The *Raleigh Register* of December 27, 1848, wrote that charity "is a luxury ... which the miserly and penurious mind can never enjoy." The editor suggested that during the Christmas season, the wealthy visit the sick and destitute in Raleigh, "administering from your abundance to their suffering and wants."

SUPERSTITIONS

Tar Heels from McDowell County thought that if 13 people sat at a table on Christmas Day, one of them would die before next Christmas. Those from Currituck County, on the other hand, thought that if 13 people sat at a table on Christmas Day, the first to rise would die before next Christmas.

In Durham County, hospitable hosts fostered the belief that for each piece of cake a person ate that was baked by someone else, one month of good luck would follow.

On January 5, called "Old Christmas Eve," cows and horses were reputed to kneel at midnight and talk to each other.

All Christmas decorations had to be removed from homes by the end of "Old Christmas," January 6, to prevent serious illness.

Entertaining a stranger in your home on Christmas Eve was thought to be a sign of much happiness during the coming year.

If a fire smoldered on Christmas Day, it was thought to betoken adversity during the coming year. If it burned brightly, it betokened prosperity.

Wearing new shoes and taking up ashes on Christmas Day

were considered unlucky.

The 12 days between Christmas and Epiphany were believed to mirror the next 12 months. A mince pie or plum pudding eaten on each of those days would ensure prosperity and good fortune to come.

Eating field peas and hog jowl on New Year's Day was thought to bring good luck.

Among Scottish settlers, the "first foot" (person) crossing the threshold on New Year's Day was thought to bring either good or ill luck for the coming year. To make the luck good, "first foot" had to bring a gift.

MORAVIANS

Much is known about Moravian Christmas celebrations because of their careful record-keeping at Old Salem. In 1762, Moravians first used lighted candles at a Christmas celebration. They don't mention having a Christmas tree, however, until 1786.

One of their most beautiful beliefs was that at midnight on Christmas Eve, cattle knelt in adoration of the Christ child. This is expressed in a Moravian Christmas song:

Good Christian men, rejoice
With heart and soul and voice.
Give ye heed to what we say:
Jesus Christ is born today!
Ox and ass before him bow,
And He is in the manger now.
Christ is born today!

— *Previously published in* The State, *December 1990.*

Christmas Prose Poem

By John G. Bragaw

Are you willing to stoop down and consider the needs and the
desires of little children;
To remember the weakness and loneliness of people who are
growing old;
To stop asking how much your friends love you, and ask
yourself whether you love them enough;
To bear in mind the things that other people have to bear on
their hearts;
To trim your lamp so that it will give more light and less smoke,
and to carry it in front of you so that your shadow will fall
behind —
Are you willing to do these things even for a day? Then you can
keep Christmas.
And if you can keep it for one day, why not always?

— *Previously published in* The State, *December 21, 1946.*